The Dragon's Tale and Other Beastly Stories

Written by Anthony Horowitz
Adapted by Trevor Baxendale
Illustrated by Simone Massoni

Published by Pearson Education Limited, Edinburgh Gate, Harlow, Essex, CM20 2JE

Registered company number: 872828

www.pearsonschools.co.uk

Adapted texts based on 'The Dragon and Saint George' from *Legends: Beasts and Monsters*, first published by Macmillan Children's Books 2010; 'Death and the Boy' from *Legends: Death and the Underworld*, first published by Macmillan's Children's Books 2011; 'The Eye of the Cyclops' from *Legends: Heroes and Villains*, first published by Macmillan's Children's Books 2011

Adaptations by Trevor Baxendale

First published 2012

16 15
10 9 8 7 6 5 4 3

British Library Cataloguing in Publication Data

A catalogue record for this book is available from the British Library

ISBN 978 0 435 07571 2

Printed and bound in Malaysia (CTP–PJB)

Acknowledgements
We would like to thank the children and teachers of Bangor Central Integrated Primary School, NI; Bishop Henderson C of E Primary School, Somerset; Brookside Community Primary School, Somerset; Cheddington Combined School, Buckinghamshire; Cofton Primary School, Birmingham; Dair House Independent School, Buckinghamshire; Deal Parochial School, Kent; Holy Trinity Catholic Primary School, Chipping Norton; Lawthorn Primry School, North Ayrshire; Newbold Riverside Primary School, Rugby and Windmill Primary School, Oxford for their invaluable help in the development and trialling of the Bug Club resources.

Every effort has been made to contact copyright holders of material reproduced in this book. Any omissions will be rectified in subsequent printings if notice is given to the publisher.

Contents

The Dragon's Tale

George

The Dragon

The King

The Princess

In ancient times, dragons were greatly feared. They usually lived in rather dank caves, often guarding huge piles of stolen treasure, and they had an unhealthy appetite for human flesh.

Saint George became famous as a dragon-killer – which is strange because he never actually killed a dragon. Although he is best known today as the patron saint of England, George was actually born in the Middle East. He was brought up by Christian parents and he travelled the world, spreading the gospel and doing good.

George's renowned encounter with the dragon happened at a small town called Silene, in Libya.

The people of Silene had lived in fear of this particular dragon for many years. They fed it two sheep every day in the vain hope that it would go away. This, of course, had exactly the opposite effect because once the dragon got used to receiving a free meal daily, it decided that the townspeople actually wanted it to remain. It hadn't the least notion that they were afraid.

Eventually, the townspeople began to run out of sheep, so all the local politicians, along with the king himself, met to find a solution.

"This is a serious situation," said one minister. "We have sacrificed all our sheep and still this dragon refuses to depart!"

The leader of the opposition got to his feet. "I have always resisted the idea of giving sheep to the dragon," he said. "If we had given it chickens, as I suggested, we would not now be facing this crisis."

"But the council's policy of giving sheep to the dragon has been a great success," another minister said. "It is true that the dragon has not gone away yet, but all the signs are that it will go away quite soon. We just need to feed it a bit more."

"If we are running out of sheep," the first minister suggested, "we could try giving it something else."

Then the king spoke, and his face was grim. "It is well known," he said, "that dragons like the taste of children. It seems to me, therefore, that there is no alternative. We must give him our children. Once a week we will feed the dragon with our sons and daughters."

For a moment, nobody spoke. The entire council was alarmed, but nobody wanted to argue with the king.

"How will we choose the children?" someone else asked.

"We will have a lottery," the king replied. "Every child in the town will be given a number. Once a week, a number will be drawn out of a hat. The child who has that number will be given to the dragon in order to save the town." He rose to his feet. "That is my law," he concluded. "There are to be no exceptions."

Three months passed, during which time a dozen children were seized by the royal guard, torn away from their weeping parents and then tied up and left outside the dragon's cave.

The dragon noticed the change in its feeding. It had been getting bored with sheep and found the children much tastier.

By the time George arrived, a dreadful atmosphere had descended on Silene. The streets were always silent on the day of the lottery. At midday a bell would ring. Soldiers would knock on the door of a house somewhere in the town and then a terrible cry of pain and despair would break the silence.

It didn't take George long to find out what was happening in Silene. He went straight to the palace to find the king, and as he walked into the throne room he heard the following conversation.

"It's out of the question!" the king was saying. "I forbid it!"

"But you gave this order," one minister replied.

"You made this law," a second said.

"And you insisted there be no exceptions," a third added.

"But she is a princess … and my daughter." Tears ran down the king's cheeks. "I was not informed that she had been designated a lottery number. When I find the idiot responsible, I'll have him executed!"

"As a matter of fact, Your Majesty," said the first minister, "it was agreed that no members of the royal family should have to draw numbers. However, your daughter took one anyway. She said she wanted to be like all the other children."

This was, in fact, the case. The princess, although she was only fourteen years old, had been horrified by the turn of events in Silene. An intelligent and educated girl, she had been one of the first to speak out against this evil lottery. When the king had refused to listen to her, she had decided to take a stand.

She had insisted on being given a number herself and, when it had been drawn, the princess had presented herself to the soldiers without any argument. Perhaps, when she was killed, her father would change his mind about this foolish law.

The king had indeed changed his mind but it was too late.

"She's already gone to the cave," the minister explained. "In fact, I'm afraid she'll already have been devoured."

"My only child!" the king wept. For the very first time, he comprehended some of the suffering of his people.

George left the palace at once, leaped on to his horse and rode out of the town in the direction of the dragon's cave.

The sound of weeping soon reached his ears. The dragon had overslept and the princess was still alive, crouched on the ground with her hands tied behind her back. George got off his horse and began to approach, but he hadn't taken more than a few steps when there was an ominous rumble from inside the cave and the dragon appeared.

When the princess saw the dragon, she closed her eyes and waited for the end. George was not deterred.

"Oh dragon!" he exclaimed. "I see you have dined well over the years. However, maybe so many free meals have clouded your judgement. Do you really mean to eat this young girl?"

The dragon growled uncertainly. The girl opened her eyes.

"God did not create people to be served up for the pleasure of wild animals," George continued. "As a creature of God, you should be ashamed of yourself. It's only because you were created by Him that I don't take out my sword and cut off your head right now. But even animals should be given a chance to repent."

Smoked trickled out the dragon's nostrils and formed a question mark.

George freed the girl and helped her to her feet. Then he took a ribbon from her dress and tied it round the dragon's neck, saying to it, "Let us go back to Silene and talk this over."

He bowed to the princess and said, "It seems to me, my lady, that you will make a much wiser and kinder ruler than your father. Your actions have demonstrated that much already."

There was a tremendous uproar in the town when George returned. First of all, the

people saw the princess walking next to him when everyone had assumed she was dead. Her obituary had already appeared in that day's newspaper. Even more astonishing was the sight of the dragon itself, walking timidly beside them at the end of a ribbon. Was this what the townspeople had been afraid of for so many years?

From that day on, nothing in Silene was the same. Indeed, by the end of the week, the entire town had converted to Christianity.

And so, in fact, had the dragon.

Shortly after that, the king retired from the throne and his daughter became queen. All the ministers were sacked and none of them was missed.

As for the dragon? It became a vegetarian and lived out its days in the palace gardens, a loyal friend and playmate of the queen's children.

Death and the Boy

Owuo

The Boy

The Brother

The Sister

Famine gripped West Africa. The water holes had dried up and the mud hardened then cracked. It was a cruel time. Every minute of every day became an exhausting struggle to find food and water while everyone prayed for rain.

In one village there was a young boy who could work no longer. He had forgotten what food tasted like, so one day, he left the village to find his fortune – or at the very least, to taste meat again.

For three days he walked without stumbling on so much as a scrap of food to eat. On the third day, just as he was about to turn round and go home again, he encountered something very peculiar.

There were forty or fifty black ropes running along the jungle floor. The boy decided to follow them.

He walked for more than a mile before the mystery was explained. The ropes weren't made of hemp. They were hair and the boy had followed them to the scalp of their owner. It was, of course, a giant. He was sitting outside a mud hut the size of a small mountain, fast asleep. Despite the famine, the giant looked remarkably well fed.

The boy was just wondering whether he should remain where he was or head for home when the giant's eyes opened.

"I didn't mean to wake you up," the boy said. "I was just searching for meat."

"If you want meat," the giant responded, "I will give it to you. But you will have to earn it by staying here and working for me."

So the boy remained, sweeping and chopping wood for the fire. In return for completing these simple tasks, the giant was true to his word and fed him with as much meat as he could eat.

There came a time, however, when the boy became homesick. It had been months since he had seen his parents and so he asked the giant for permission to take a short holiday.

"Of course," the giant said, "but you must send me a substitute while you're gone."

"I'll do that," the boy promised, and he set off through the jungle.

The boy's family was delighted to see him when he got back and were astonished to find him looking so plump and healthy. His brother in particular questioned him about what had happened.

"If you really want to know, I can help you," the boy told him. "How would you like a job where in return for the lightest of tasks you got more meat than you knew what to do with?"

"I'd love it!" the brother said.

The boy told him about the giant and his brother leaped at the opportunity to take his place.

"By the way," he asked, just before he left, "what is this giant of yours called?"

"His name is Owuo," the boy said.

Now Owuo is a West African word, and it means 'death'.

Six weeks passed; more than enough time to cure the boy's homesickness. The trouble with home was that there still wasn't any meat and worse still, his parents expected him to join in the household chores. This meant far harder work than the boy had got used to with Owuo. So one day, he left the village and followed the path of hair back to the giant's hut.

He had expected to see his brother there but to his surprise there was no sign of him. The giant, however, was untroubled.

"He left a couple of days ago," he explained. "I'm surprised you didn't cross paths with him in the jungle."

"I thought he'd have waited for me," the boy said, puzzled.

Time passed as it had before. The giant seemed perfectly content even though the boy did precious little work. Meanwhile, the boy consumed so much meat that he became quite fat, but once again, the only problem was that he missed his family. So he asked the giant if he could be allowed a second holiday.

"Very well!" the giant said. "Except this time I wonder if you could send me a young girl to take your place? I have it in mind to take a wife. If you could rustle up a pretty girl, I'd like to marinate … I mean, marry her."

The boy returned to his village again. This time he was greeted with a little less pleasure. For despite what the giant had said, his brother had never returned home.

The boy still didn't mention the giant. It was only when he was talking to his sister one evening that he mentioned Owuo, and in particular his desire for a wife.

"A wife?" his sister repeated. "If I were the wife of this Owuo, I would never have to work again. Like you, I could eat meat all day long."

"Yes, but …" the boy began uncertainly.

"How do I find him?" the sister interrupted.

Although the boy felt uneasy about it, his sister forced him to describe the path of hair, and the next morning she left.

This time the boy only waited a fortnight before he followed her back to the giant's hut. It was with a sinking feeling that he found Owuo sitting by himself, gnawing a bone.

"You're back early," the giant said.

"Yes," the boy replied. "My sister ...?"

"I haven't seen her for a week." The giant tossed the bone over his shoulder. "I expect she'll turn up soon. Get yourself some supper, my boy. You must be hungry after your journey."

The boy wasn't hungry, but nodding his thanks, he went into the giant's hut. As always, the ground was littered with bones and it was as he stepped over these that he stopped. His eyes bulged. His hair stood on end.

There was a bracelet made of red beads around one of the bones. He would have recognised it anywhere, for he had made it himself. He had given it to his sister as a birthday present.

That night, as soon as it was dark, the boy tiptoed away from the hut and with his heart pounding, raced through the jungle. He didn't stop until he had reached his village where, breathlessly, he told his parents what had happened.

Angry and afraid, the villagers marched into the jungle, carrying with them flaming torches to light their way. The boy accompanied them, for he knew that he was to blame, and there was nothing he would not do to make amends.

It was by the light of the torches that they came upon the hair, more like snakes than

rope now as it twisted through the night. Then the boy had an idea.

"Owuo is too big for us to fight," he cried. "Let the fire do our work for us."

With that, the boy seized a torch and thrust it into the hair.

Like a burning fuse, the hair hissed and crackled, carrying the fire on a winding path through the jungle. The villagers followed close behind and they arrived at the hut just in time to see Owuo erupt in flames. One moment he was sleeping peacefully; the next he had disappeared in a screaming inferno. Then it was all over, and only a great heap of ash showed where he had lain.

However, rummaging around in the ashes, the boy came upon a small bottle that Owuo had kept hidden in the very hair that had been his undoing. There were just three drops of a transparent liquid in the bottle.

Realising that whatever it was must be magic, the boy allowed two of the drops to fall onto the bones in the giant's hut. In an instant, to the great rejoicing of the villagers, his brother and sister sprang to life, apparently none the worse for having been chewed up, swallowed and digested.

"Now – what shall I do with the last drop?" the boy asked.

"Wait!" his father said.

"No!" his mother cried.

For the boy had upturned the bottle over the ashes of the giant.

Everyone stared.

A puddle formed in the middle of the ashes, bubbling and hissing. Slowly, hideously, an eye took shape. It opened, then gazed balefully at the boy who staggered back, terrified.

But that was all. Although the potion was powerful enough to restore a human life, it could manage no more than one eye of the giant.

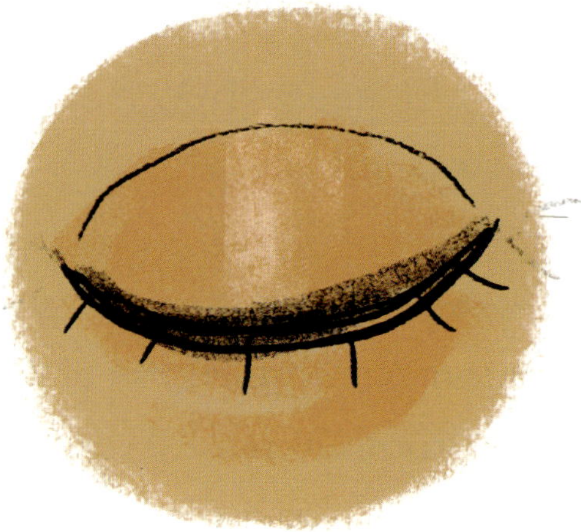

In Togo, where this myth originated, the people believe that the eye is still there, and that whenever it blinks, someone, somewhere in the world, dies. Because there is so much dust in the country, it blinks often. And one day, they say, the eye will blink for you ...

The Eye of the Cyclops

Polyphemus

Odysseus

The Cyclops was a terrifying creature. It was the size of a house with thick, curly hair, a filthy beard and only one eye, set in the middle of its forehead. It was very ugly, extremely bad-tempered and violent. Any good book of Greek myths will tell you this. What is less often mentioned is the fact that the Cyclops was also incredibly stupid.

The most famous Cyclops was called Polyphemus. He had settled on an island in the middle of the Aegean Sea where he lived in a cave and looked after a flock of sheep.

Polyphemus had no friends but he knew all his sheep by name. He chatted to them, milked them as gently as his huge fingers could manage and shed tears whenever he had to slaughter one in order to make lamb stew.

One day, Polyphemus was astonished to find that he had visitors. They were sitting in front of his fire and feasting on one of his sheep. There were about a dozen of them and, looking more closely, he was delighted to see that they were human beings.

Polyphemus loved human beings in his own way – which was either cooked or raw. He particularly liked the way their bones crunched between his teeth but didn't stick in his throat.

The Cyclops' face lit up in a great smile. It was also a horrible smile for, having just one eye in the middle of his forehead, everything he did with his face was horrible.

"Who are you?" he demanded.

The men huddled together in terror. Then one of them stepped forward.

“Good monster,” he said, “we are Greeks. We are returning home having fought a great war at Troy. We stopped here to find fresh provisions for our ship and thought we might pass the night in your cave.”

Polyphemus scowled. He had never heard of Troy and didn’t particularly like being addressed as ‘monster’.

The man bowed low. “I am sure you need no reminding,” he said, “of the laws of Zeus, which demand hospitality to poor travellers such as ourselves …”

Unfortunately, the man was wasting his time. Polyphemus didn't even know what 'hospitality' meant. Moreover, he was hungry. His mouth had been watering from the moment he had seen the human beings. Now, brushing the man aside, he grabbed two of his companions and tossed them into his mouth. Crunch! Crunch! He shivered with pleasure as they slid down his throat. If he had two for breakfast and another two for dinner every day, they

would last him until … It was no good, the sum was too difficult for Polyphemus. Instead, he rolled a huge stone in front of the cave's entrance to trap the men inside, and fell into a contented sleep.

Now the men in the cave were, as their leader had said, Greek warriors returning home from ten long years of war. Their leader was called Odysseus and he was to become one of the most celebrated of all the Greek heroes.

Odysseus was the King of Ithaca, and he was already well-known for his cunning and trickery. There seemed little he could do at the moment, however. The stone that the Cyclops had rolled across the entrance to the cave was far too big to move.

The following morning, when the giant woke up, Odysseus could only watch helplessly as two more of his men were seized and devoured. Then the giant left, herding his sheep in front of him, and at last Odysseus was able to set his mind to work.

Polyphemus kept a plentiful supply of wood for his fire and each log was the size of a small tree. Odysseus ordered his men to draw their swords and together they began hacking at one of the logs. It took hours but by the time evening arrived, they had removed all the branches, cut the tip to a needle-sharp point and hidden the whole thing at the back of the cave.

When the stone rolled aside at dusk, the sheep came in and behind them came Polyphemus. Two more of the unfortunate travellers disappeared into the giant's mouth but this time, before Polyphemus could fall asleep, Odysseus approached him.

"Sweet monster," he cried, "I hope you have enjoyed my two friends."

"They were a bit chewy," Polyphemus replied.

"That was probably their armour," said Odysseus. "Anyway, I was wondering if you would care to quench your thirst with some wine after your delicious supper."

"What's wine?" the Cyclops asked.

"It is a drink made from grapes, O mighty one," Odysseus explained. "By chance, I have some with me here ..."

He gestured towards two barrels, which held enough wine for twenty men. Polyphemus snatched one up and drank the whole lot down in one mouthful.

"It's good!" he exclaimed. "Do you have more?"

"One more barrel, your greatness," Odysseus said.

Polyphemus grabbed the second barrel and drank that one down too. But the wine was very strong and the giant became rather drunk.

"Washernem?" he asked.

"I beg your pardon?" Odysseus said.

"Your name? Wash your name?"

"It is Oudeis," Odysseus told him, explaining that this was the Greek word for 'nobody'.

"Nobody?" Polyphemus repeated. "Well … Nobody is my friend, and because he's my friend, I'll eat Nobody last of all. I'll eat all the others first. Then Nobody after."

On that note, Polyphemus fell into a drunken slumber.

At once, Odysseus and his men lifted up the log they had prepared and climbed onto the Cyclops' chest. But Polyphemus awoke and began to scream the place down when the men drove the wooden stake right into his eye. The Greek warriors raced to the back of the cave as he leaped up and down, bellowing so loudly that several other Cyclopes gathered round the mouth of the cave and demanded to know what was going on.

"I am blinded and in ghastly pain," Polyphemus moaned.

"How did it happen?" one of the Cyclopes called out.

"It was Nobody's fault," Polyphemus explained.

"You mean … it was an accident?"

"No! No! Nobody did it to me. I blame Nobody. In fact, I'm going to kill Nobody on account of it."

The Cyclopes looked at one another and scratched their heads.

"If nobody's done anything," they said at last, "you must be having a bad dream. Why don't you just go back to sleep and give us some peace?"

With that, they turned their backs on the cave and went back to bed.

The following morning found Polyphemus in a miserable state. Everything was dark for him and he had a blinding headache. Nonetheless, he rolled the stone aside to let his flock out to pasture, taking great care to feel each animal with his hands in case any of the men tried to escape.

This was what Odysseus had been waiting for. During the course of the night, he had tied some of the sheep together with their own long wool. Then, in exactly the same way, he had tied his surviving men underneath them, so that they hung just above the ground. Although the blinded giant ran his hands along the backs of the sheep, he didn't think to feel underneath them, and so that way, the Greeks were able to escape.

The prisoners reached their ship and set sail as quickly as they could. As they left, Odysseus couldn't help laughing and called out to the giant.

"If anyone asks who blinded you, tell them it was Odysseus, King of Ithaca. Perhaps the next time strangers call, you will remember the sacred laws of hospitality!"

Unsurprisingly, Polyphemus never did show anyone the slightest trace of hospitality. He spent the rest of his days sitting in the fields with his sheep, moaning to himself.

And who can blame him?